Facilitating Success

Group Communication Skills for Enhanced Collaboration

Table of Contents

Chapter 1. Introduction

Unlock the full potential of your team with our comprehensive Special Report: "Facilitating Success: Group Communication Skills for Enhanced Collaboration". This energizing resource doesn't only highlight why effective group communication is vital in today's fast-paced world, but it provides practical strategies, innovative techniques, and actionable insights, turning collaboration from a buzzword into a key competitive advantage. Whether you're a start-up finding its footing, a large corporation seeking to refresh remote team dynamics, or an individual aiming to boost your collaboration skills, this report is a roadmap to taking your team's performance and workplace satisfaction to new heights. Don't wait, embark on this transformative journey today for more effective, efficient, and rewarding group interactions!

Chapter 2. The Power of Effective Group Communication

In an era of digital transformation and constant change, effective group communication stands at the core of successful team functioning. Not only does it foster understanding, but it also aids in the resolution of issues, boosts team morale, and fuels innovation.

2.1. Understanding Group Communication

Group communication refers to interactions among individuals where most information, ideas and thoughts are shared. It could range from an informal chat between team members to structured meetings, conference calls, or email threads. From decision-making to problem-solving, group communication underpins every aspect of teamwork. The better the team communicates, the more they can harness their individual capabilities to drive collective success.

2.2. Significance of Group Communication

Effective communication in a group setting performs several vital functions. It facilitates information exchange, promotes understanding and emotional connection among individuals, contributes to identity formation within the group, and aids in decision-making and problem-solving processes.

More significantly, it can enhance team performance by:

1. **Boosting Productivity**: Idle gossip harms productivity, while effective communication can promote it. Every team member working on a shared objective should understand their role and how they contribute to the overall goal. Clear, concise, and effective communication helps create a picture of what success looks like, accelerating productivity.

2. **Improving Morale**: Communication impacts team morale significantly. Expressing personal experiences, challenges, and accomplishments can create a supportive work environment. Employees who feel heard and appreciated are more likely to feel motivated about their work.

3. **Nurturing Innovation**: Ideas flourish in an environment that encourages open dialogue. Effective group communication cultivates an open environment where every team member feels valued and their opinions respected, fostering an innovative mindset and encouraging creative exploration.

2.3. Barriers to Effective Group Communication

Identifying the hurdles hampering efficient communication in a group is the first step to creating a stable communication pathway. Common barriers could be:

1. **Ambiguous Language**: Vague or overly complex language can create misunderstandings. Simplifying the language and ensuring clarity can promote effective communication.

2. **Physical Distractions**: Noisy meeting rooms or malfunctioning technology can disrupt the flow of communication. Creating a conducive environment with adequate infrastructural support can facilitate unhindered communication.

3. **Emotional Biases**: Personal biases or emotional walls can hinder open dialogue. Promoting emotional intelligence within the team

can encourage honest, unfiltered conversations.

4. **Information Overload**: An excess of information can be as crippling as the lack of it. Defining the necessary information and moderating its flow can produce effective interactions.

2.4. Enhancing Group Communication

Transforming the communication ethos of a team needs concerted effort. Several strategies can help enhance group communication dynamics.

1. **Promote Active Listening**: Active listening ensures everyone fully understands what is being said. Encourage team members to subdue their personal biases, understand the speaker's perspective, and provide thoughtful feedback.

2. **Use Collaborative Tools**: Leveraging modern technology can greatly enhance team communication. Online platforms like Slack or Microsoft Teams help collate team conversations and organize dialogues by topics, fostering structured and efficient communication.

3. **Encourage Transparency**: Encourage an environment where individuals can express themselves freely. Transparency fosters trust, a fundamental requirement for efficient teamwork.

4. **Develop a Feedback Culture**: Constructive feedback can help individuals understand their areas of improvement. Regular feedback sessions can promote consistent growth and improvement.

2.5. Conclusion

The power of effective group communication is immense. When harnessed correctly, it can boost productivity, enhance morale, and stimulate innovation. However, it invariably requires mindful effort, patience, and adaptability from each member. Implementing effective group communication practices and continuously seeking to improve upon them will lead the team towards unprecedented success.

Don't underestimate the power of communication — it is the very essence of effective teamwork and can be the key to unlocking your team's full potential.

Chapter 3. Understanding Different Communication Styles

Effective communication acts as the keystone for successful collaboration in any team, be it small startups or large corporations. If executed well, it can enhance overall productivity, build trust, and improve relationships among team members. One important facet deserving deep exploration in this broad subject is understanding and leveraging different communication styles. By recognizing and adapting to these styles, we can create a platform for clearer, more efficient and harmonious exchanges within our teams.

3.1. Layers of Communication

Most people have a dominant mode of communication to express thoughts and ideas. Clarity and understanding of the following four layers of communication can help manage diversity in communication styles.

1. Verbal: includes the use of words, either spoken or written. The focus is on the clear expression of thoughts and ideas using language.

2. Non-verbal: is expressed through body language, posture, facial expressions or gestures. It can be intentional or unintentional and often complements or contradicts verbal messages.

3. Listening: involves the attention given to others when they're talking. Active listening is a key aspect that shows a person is engaged and interested.

4. Emotional: centers around how people express their feelings. It can influence or be influenced by the attitude, perceptions, or

reactions of those who are communicating.

Recognizing these layers is the first step to understanding different communication styles. It's crucial to remember that every individual might have different degrees and combinations of these communication layers.

3.2. The Four Communication Styles

Based on multiple research studies, communication styles can be broadly classified into four categories based on how individuals give and receive information: 1. Passive, 2. Aggressive, 3. Passive-Aggressive, 4. Assertive.

1. Passive: This style is characterized by the individual's reluctance to express their thoughts and feelings. Passive communicators often go to great lengths to avoid conflict and have a tendency to agree to things they may not actually want.

2. Aggressive: This style is at the other end of the spectrum. Aggressive communicators regularly voice their opinions, even at the risk of offending others. While they are clear about their wants and needs, they often overlook the needs and feelings of others.

3. Passive-Aggressive: This style is complex and can be harder to identify. Passive-aggressive communicators seem passive on the surface but may act out in subtle, indirect or behind-the-scenes ways.

4. Assertive: This is often considered the most effective and balanced communication style. Assertive communicators articulate their thoughts and feelings openly and honestly, respect the thoughts and feelings of others, and look for compromise and resolution in conflict situations.

3.3. Active Listening - A Guiding Tool

Despite the range of communication styles, there is one tool that can guide anyone to better communication: active listening. This involves hearing out the other party completely, acknowledging their message, providing feedback, and postponing your judgment.

Here are a few tips to hone your active listening skills:

- Show that you are listening through your body language

- Echo the speaker's message to show understanding

- Ask clarifying questions if needed

- Summarize the key points after the speaker finishes

- Give feedback to validate the speaker's thoughts and feelings

3.4. Strategies for Communicating with Different Styles

1. When interacting with passive communicators, encourage participation and make them feel safe to express their thoughts and feelings.

2. When dealing with aggressive communicators, maintain your composure and assert your needs and feelings respectfully.

3. Uncovering the underlying issues with passive-aggressive communicators can be challenging. Be patient, promote open dialogue and express concerns directly but tactfully.

4. With assertive communicators, engage in open, balanced discussions. Emphasize respect and cooperation.

3.5. Reflecting on Your Communication Style

Recognizing your own preferred communication style can increase your self-awareness and improve your interactions with others. This understanding can help you adapt when interacting with others with different styles, leading to more effective communication.

3.6. Concluding Remarks

Understanding different communication styles and honing our abilities to adapt as per the situation can pave the way for enhanced group collaboration. While the transition might not happen overnight, the journey will no doubt result in improved team morale, productivity, and overall success. Remember, successful communication is not merely about transferring information but also about understanding the emotions behind the information. Keep striving to be a better communicator – it's a journey, not a destination.

Chapter 4. Building Trust within Teams: The Foundation of Communication

Any team's ability to function successfully is deeply rooted in trust. Trust refers to the confidence among team members about the character, ability, strength, or truth of each other. It's an essential element, underscoring all aspects of collaborative efforts from the straightforward sharing of responsibilities to complex group decision-making processes. Let's explore how to create a culture of trust within teams effectively.

4.1. Understanding Trust

Trust doesn't happen overnight; it's cultivated over time through consistent interactions. A lack of trust can lead to misunderstanding and conflict, hindering a team's opportunity for achieving collective success. Trust streamlines communication, fosters cooperation, and spurs innovation and problem-solving. By establishing trust, you're not focusing on makeshift solutions or passing trends in team management, but laying down the foundation of a resilient, robust, and unified team.

4.2. The Importance of Building Trust

Trust is not merely a soft social construct. It's indeed a hard, measurable economic driver. Google's Project Aristotle showed that psychological safety, a sense of confidence that the team will not embarrass or punish anyone for speaking up, was crucial to successful teams more than anything else. This psychological safety is imbued and fostered through trust.

When individuals in a team trust each other, they are more likely to: . Share thoughts, ideas, and information openly . Provide and accept feedback gracefully . Support each other in achieving common objectives . Feel comfortable taking calculated risks . Commit to team decisions and actions

4.3. Establishing Trust: Key Techniques

Building trust within a team is not happenstance but a deliberate effort. Indeed, it requires consistent effort, time, and patience. Here are some invaluable strategies to create a trusting environment:

1. **Clear Communication**: Unclear communication can breed misunderstanding and confusion — fertile grounds for mistrust. Effective communication reduces ambiguity and ensures everyone on the team understands their role, tasks, and expectations. Leaders should also maintain an open dialogue about the team's progress and challenges.

2. **Transparency**: Team leaders should practice open transparency in operations and decision-making processes. When team members feel included and understand why specific decisions are made, trust will grow.

3. **Consistency**: Consistent actions and decisions from team leaders create a predictable and comfortable environment where trust can thrive. This includes following up on promises and treating each team member fairly.

4. **Showing Vulnerability**: By admitting mistakes and acknowledging the need for help, team leaders show their vulnerability. This demonstration prompts other team members

to act in kind, promoting an environment of mutual trust.

5. **Recognition and Appreciation**: Recognizing the contributions of team members is essential for building trust. Team leaders must acknowledge the effort made by their teammates, no matter how small.

4.4. Overcoming Trust Barriers

Despite the best efforts, there might be instances when teams face trust issues. Some common trust barriers are unrealized expectations, unresolved conflicts, and lack of accountability. Turning these barriers into opportunities for building trust can enhance team performance and cohesion.

1. **Addressing Expectations**: Expectations should be explicitly discussed, aligned, and managed from the outset. Unrealized expectations can lead to disappointment and mistrust.

2. **Resolving Conflicts**: An unaddressed conflict can erode trust over time. Timely and open communication, understanding, and empathy are critical for dealing with conflicts in a positive manner that strengthens trust.

3. **Fostering Accountability**: When team members don't take responsibility for their actions, trust begins to crumble. To maintain and build trust, it's important to create an environment that encourages honesty, openness, and responsibility for individual and team actions.

Trust, the undercurrent of successful collaboration, does not grow in a vacuum. It requires honesty, respect, understanding, and mutual cooperation from all the team members. As we foster these attributes, we contribute to building and maintaining a strong foundation of trust that can withstand the pressures of demanding projects, tight deadlines, and high-stakes decisions. And with that trust in place, we can truly begin to unlock the full potential of our teams.

Chapter 5. The Role of Active Listening in Collaborative Environments

Active listening, a multifaceted skill positioned at the heart of effective communication, is often compared to a mirror reflecting both a speaker's words and underlying elements such as feelings or intentions. This communication technique, highlighting the necessity of full engagement and empathetic response from the listener, is essential in fostering collaboration and team cohesion.

5.1. The Cornerstones of Active Listening

Active listening goes beyond simply hearing the words that are spoken. It requires complete focus, understanding, response, and the application of non-verbal cues. These four stages form the bedrock of active listening.

1. Focusing: Staying in the moment and minimizing distractions lay the foundation for active listening. Electronically, physically, or mentally distancing oneself from other tasks and focusing solely on the speaker is the first step.

2. Understanding: The second step involves interpreting the message, its gist, and nuances. Comprehension is vital, so if anything remains unclear, the listener should ask for clarification.

3. Responding: This step involves constructive feedback, showing the speaker that the listener has understood their point of view and respected their sentiments.

4. Non-verbal cues: Lastly, the listener should employ appropriate

body language, like maintaining eye contact and open body posture, to non-verbally indicate interest and engagement.

5.2. The Role of Active Listening in Knowledge Sharing

Effective knowledge sharing is predicated on understanding and trust, which are achieved through active listening. In a collaborative environment, individuals exchange specialized knowledge and experiences, refining collective understanding and problem-solving capabilities.

Often, crucial information is tacit, embedded in personal experiences or local contexts. Active listening helps elicit such knowledge, turning personal insights into shared wisdom. It fosters open dialogue, eases communication of complex ideas, and aids in contextual understanding, which collectively lead to the synthesis of shared knowledge.

5.3. Active Listening as A Bridge to Empathy

Empathy breeds trust and mutual respect, underpinning collaborative synergy. Active listening, by demonstrating genuine interest and understanding, fosters empathetic connections. When people feel heard, they tend to reciprocate the respect and openness they have received. The resultant string of empathetic communications can do wonders for creating a harmonious, collaborative environment.

5.4. Active Listening towards Conflict Management

Conflicts can derail collaboration, but active listening can prevent misunderstandings from snowballing or ameliorate existing disputes. It affirms each party's perspectives, validates their emotions, and promotes mutual understanding. By facilitating empathetic exchanges, active listening sparks meaningful dialogues that help peers reconcile their differences, thus mitigating conflicts and facilitating productive interactions.

5.5. Facilitating Dialogues and Decision-making

Active listening helps structure dialogues, shaping them into productive, future-oriented discussions. By ensuring that every participant feels heard, it propels equitable decision-making. This significantly affects the ownership and commitment levels of the team towards the decision, alleviating implementation roadblocks.

5.6. Active Listening as the Key to Personal Growth

Active Listening also channels personal growth, fostering self-awareness and emotional intelligence. It offers opportunities to understand diverse perspectives and ideas, boosting creativity and problem-solving skills.

5.7. Developing Active Listening Habits

Active listening can be cultivated by shedding passive listening habits. This involves mitigating distractions, practicing mindfulness, asking probing questions, providing feedback, and honing non-verbal communication skills. A conscious effort is required initially, but with practice, it can become second nature.

5.8. The Challenges of Active Listening

While understanding the importance of active listening, implementing it consistently poses challenges. These may include preconceived notions, attention deficits, or communication noise. However, with perseverance and regular practice, these obstacles can be overcome, ensuring that active listening becomes a critical tool in a team's collaborative arsenal.

5.9. In Conclusion: Active Listening as a Crucial Skill for Collaboration

Active listening is not a mere technique, but a philosophy of engaging in genuine dialogues, fostering understanding, empathy, and trust. It is a crucial skill for effective collaboration that can significantly impact team performance and decision-making, serving as a potent ingredient for success in collaborative environments. With patience, practice, and commitment, active listening can be mastered, impelling both individual and collective growth.

Chapter 6. Conflict Management for Enhanced Collaboration

Understanding that Conflict is Inevitable

In any group dynamic, whether it's a sports team or an office team, conflict is inevitable. A diversity of backgrounds, experiences, and perspectives can lead to contradictions, differences in opinions, and ultimately conflict. However, rather than seeing this as a negative, it should be seen as an opportunity for growth and learning. Conflict is not inherently negative; it can be a stepping stone to finding better solutions and improving group cohesion, provided it is handled correctly.

6.1. The Types of Conflict

There are generally three types of conflict that may surface within a group:

1. Team Conflict This typically occurs when there is disagreement among team members about decisions and direction. If left unaddressed, these disagreements can escalate, resulting in lowered productivity and morale.

2. Role Conflict This occurs when there is unclear or overlapping roles and responsibilities among team members. It can create uncertainty and frustration, and can hinder collaboration.

3. Personality Conflict Clashes arising from differing personality styles can be complicated and have significant impact on team dynamics.

Each type of conflict needs appropriate remediation, and

understanding the origin is the first step in making a constructive approach to resolution.

6.2. The Role of Effective Communication in Conflict Resolution

One of the most important skills for managing conflicts is effective communication. Listening actively to understand team members' perspectives, expressing opinions constructively, and giving and receiving feedback respectfully are all foundational elements of communication that facilitate conflict resolution. Moreover, understanding non-verbal communication, such as body language and facial expressions, is crucial, as they can often reveal more about a person's feelings than their words.

6.3. Tools and Techniques for Conflict Resolution

Several approaches to conflict resolution have proven effective, and knowing which to apply in a given situation can drastically improve the outcome.

1. The Thomas-Kilmann Model Developed by Kenneth Thomas and Ralph Kilmann, this conflict resolution model outlines five strategies: competing, avoiding, accommodating, compromising, and collaborating. The choice of strategy depends on the nature of the conflict, its intensity, and the relationships involved.

2. Mediation In complex situations where the parties involved are unable to reach a resolution, the intervention of a neutral third party may be necessary. A mediator can help facilitate dialogue and guide the team towards a mutually acceptable resolution.

3. Conflict Resolution Training Regular training for employees on conflict resolution can help prevent many disagreements from escalating.

Each of these techniques requires practice and patience - no single approach will work every time. However, making a commitment to understand and resolve conflicts can drastically improve team collaboration.

6.4. Building a Culture of Constructive Conflict

Developing a positive, constructive approach to conflict within a team can help to prevent disagreements from escalating into unproductive confrontations. There are several strategies that can help build this culture:

1. Respect Differences Encourage team members to appreciate their potential conflicts as opportunities for growth and learning.

2. Encourage Open Conversations Create an environment where team members feel safe expressing their opinions, even if they are contrary to others'.

3. Establish Clear Roles Clearly define each team member's roles and responsibilities, which can help reduce misunderstandings and role conflict.

4. Develop Conflict Resolution Processes Having standard processes in place for managing and mediating conflicts will ensure they're handled consistently and fairly.

Such strategies can turn potential disagreements into sources of creativity and emergence of revolutionary ideas.

6.5. Leading by Example

Leaders play a key role in conflict management by setting an example and modeling appropriate behavior. They can foster constructive conflict by encouraging open communication, respecting different viewpoints, and displaying empathy. Also, by intervening swiftly and judiciously when conflicts do arise, leaders can ensure that conflicts are resolved in a positive way.

By understanding and appreciating the inevitability of conflict in teams, and by practicing effective conflict resolution strategies, leaders and team members alike can improve the overall team performance. Conflict doesn't have to be something to fear or avoid; instead, it can be a tool for learning, growth, and progress, when managed correctly. Conflict management is a crucial skill, and mastering it can vastly improve the quality of team coordination, collaboration, and overall satisfaction.

Chapter 7. Leveraging Technology in Group Communication

In the 21st-century corporate milieu, leveraging technology has become intricately entwined with all facets of group communication. When wielded deftly, digital tools can catalyze efficient information exchange, streamline collaboration, and engender a more inclusive, engaging, and productive environment.

7.1. The Advent of Digital Technologies

With the progression of technology from the early-age emails and teleconferencing to the contemporary advanced collaborative digital tools, we've embarked on an era where virtual communication can be as effective as face-to-face interactions, if not more. These tools extend beyond mere communication and offer a plethora of services such as cloud-based storage, workflow management, and brainstorming tools, thereby ensuring a seamless communication line that is efficient, sustainable, and cost-effective.

Traditional communicative models often restricted creativity and engagement due to geographical boundaries and asynchronous information exchange. Current technologies, however, have redefined this paradigm, ushering in an age of inclusivity and unprecedented ease of communication.

Despite this, it is crucial not to get overwhelmed by the glut of technologies available and instead identify which ones best suit your team's needs. Assessing factors such as availability of tech support, customization options, ease of use, security measures, and integration capabilities will provide insights into the right tool for your team.

7.2. Choosing the Right Communication Tool

Effective team communication thrives on the right blend of synchronous (real-time) and asynchronous (not real-time) communications. While video meeting tools like Zoom and Google Meet foster real-time collaboration, platforms like Slack, MS teams, or email cater to asynchronous communication by allowing team members to respond in their own time.

But before choosing your communication tools, it's crucial to define your objectives clearly. What are you trying to facilitate – fast response times? Accumulative brainstorming? Task delegation? Each goal may warrant a different application.

7.3. Integrating Social Media

It's important not to overlook social media in a business communication plan. Networking platforms like LinkedIn, Facebook, or Twitter can enhance intra-team rapport and aid in establishing a robust professional network. Furthermore, they allow an organization to have a wider reach and display thought leadership by sharing industry insights and company content.

However, the use of social media should be moderated. Policies need to be in place to ensure its effective and appropriate use, safeguarding against misinformation and any potential PR pitfalls.

7.4. Deciphering Email Communication

Even in the era of advanced digital tools, emails continue to form an integral part of professional communication. Though encumbered by delayed responses and the risk of being misconstrued, emails are unparalleled in communicating detailed information, preserving a record, and maintaining professionalism.

Teams can enhance their email communication by incorporating a few practices. A clear and concise subject line aids in capturing attention. Timely responses, use of professional language, and maintaining email etiquette like answering all questions posed, acknowledging receipt, and proofreading before sending can improve the quality of email interaction.

7.5. Utilizing Collaborative Tools

With mounting complexities in today's projects, simple communication tools often fall short. Enter collaborative tools: from file sharing tools like Google Drive, OneDrive, to project management software like Trello, Asana, and collaborative content creation tools like Google Docs and Notion - their utility is multifold.

For success in this arena, teams should look to use tools that allow easy access to project information, updates in real-time, integration with other tools, and customization to fit the team's specific needs. Regular training sessions can help members stay up-to-date with the latest features and use the tools optimally.

7.6. Harnessing Video Conferencing

Video conferencing platforms have played a pivotal role in sustaining remote work dynamics. They have connected teams spread across the globe, facilitating brainstorming sessions, meetings, webinars, and fostering a sense of community.

They make communication more effective by providing visual cues, making interaction more personal than textual or audio communication. Tools like Zoom, Microsoft Teams, or Webex Meetings offer features like screen sharing, virtual whiteboards, and breakout rooms, further enhancing the team's collaborative potential.

7.7. Navigating Digital Etiquette

In the digital communication landscape, adhering to digital etiquette is paramount. This includes ensuring prompt responses, respecting time zones for virtual meetings, using professional language, and respecting privacy.

Also, understanding that text-based communication lacks non-verbal cues, it's important to articulate messages clearly and unambiguously. Using emojis, where suitable, can portray emotions and thus prevent misinterpretation. Ethical use of technology, like refraining from unnecessary email forwarding, respecting copyright laws, and maintaining online safety practices is part of the digital etiquette too.

7.8. Addressing Cybersecurity

As the reliance on digital communication increases, so does the need for potent cybersecurity measures. The paradigm shift in work culture towards remote operations has opened avenues for cyber threats.

Encryption of confidential communication, use of secure and reliable platforms, awareness and adherence to cybersecurity policies, use of two-factor authentication, and having strong, unique passwords are a few measures that can be undertaken to mitigate this risk. Regular team briefings on the latest threats and best practices to overcome them can further fortify your team's cyber defenses.

In conclusion, digital tools, when optimally leveraged, have the potential to redefine the avenues of team communication. As we stride deeper into the digital era, the focus must also be on integrating these tools with emotional intelligence to create a harmonious coexistence between technology and human needs in team communication.

Chapter 8. Practices for Effective Remote Team Communication

The landscape of the modern workplace is rapidly shifting, with remote work no longer an anomaly but a predominant mode of operation in many companies. As such, ensuring effective communication in remote teams has become critical. This chapter aims to provide comprehensive and practical strategies for enhancing remote team communication.

8.1. Establish Clear and Consistent Communication Channels

Establishing clear and consistent communication channels is the foundation of efficient remote team communication. Different tools serve different communication needs. Email may be favored for asynchronous communication and documenting important discussions, while instant messaging platforms like Slack or Microsoft Teams can facilitate real-time communication and foster a more relaxed atmosphere.

Video conferencing tools, such as Zoom or Google Meet, enable visual interaction, which can be crucial for complex discussions or those requiring non-verbal cues. Project management tools like Asana and Trello can help communicate tasks and deadlines.

For these tools to foster constructive communication, however, they need to be used consistently by the team. Set team norms on which tools to use for specific types of communication. Make all team members aware of these norms and ensure they have the necessary training and equipment to utilize them effectively.

8.2. Conduct Regular Check-Ins and Meetings

Conducting regular check-ins and meetings is pivotal to keeping everyone on the same page. Team meetings help maintain collective focus on project goals and enable team members to raise concerns or provide updates on their tasks. One-on-one check-ins offer a platform for team members to share personal challenges that may affect their performance or require adjustments to work assignment.

In scheduling these meetings, be mindful of time zones if working with a globally distributed team. All team members should feel equally considered and able to contribute.

8.3. Promoting Open Communication

Promoting an environment of open communication is vital in a remote setting. This means encouraging all team members to voice their ideas, concerns, and feedback. This can be achieved through regular feedback sessions, fostering a culture of appreciating diverse views, and ensuring team leaders are approachable and responsive.

An open communication culture can significantly contribute to problem-solving and innovation as it promotes the sharing and discussing of new ideas. Consequently, it builds trust and fosters a climate of mutual support and collaboration.

8.4. Utilize Collaborative Tools

Leveraging collaborative tools can significantly boost productivity in remote teams. Tools like Google Docs allow team members to work on documents simultaneously, showcasing progress in real-time and promoting a sense of collaboration. Shared digital whiteboards can facilitate brainstorming sessions, while tools like GitHub can streamline coding for software development teams.

These tools not only enhance the collaborative experience but they also make tracking progress and providing feedback easy and timely. Training in using these tools effectively should be part of the onboarding process for new team members and ongoing professional development for existing ones.

8.5. Managing Communication Overload

While constant communication is pivotal, it can also lead to information overload, reducing its effectiveness. Therefore, it is vital to manage communication load by differentiating between critical updates that require immediate attention and less urgent matters that can be addressed asynchronously.

Also, a few well-structured, concise messages are often better than a series of disorganized notes. This simplifies communication, making it less time-consuming and more effective.

8.6. Ensuring Multicultural Sensitivity

With remote work enabling teams to span across different regions and cultures, it's crucial to ensure cultural sensitivity in communication. Cultural awareness training can help to avoid multicultural misunderstandings and make all team members feel valued and included.

8.7. Building and Maintaining Trust

Building and maintaining trust in a remote setting can be challenging but it's a crucial component of effective communication. This can be fostered through consistency in communication, setting and meeting expectations, providing constructive feedback, and showing empathy and understanding.

8.8. Empowering Success Through Asynchronous Communication

Asynchronous communication can be powerful in avoiding disruptions and accommodating diverse schedules within a remote team. Providing opportunities for asynchronous communication - like the use of email, discussion boards or collaborative documents - can allow all team members to contribute in their own time, leading to more thoughtful responses and inclusive discussions.

In conclusion, while remote work presents its challenges, with the right practices, tools, and mindset, effective team communication can be achieved. This requires not only understanding and leveraging advanced tools but also fostering key interpersonal skills and attitudes, such as cultural sensitivity, open communication, and trust. As we navigate this new era of remote work, these practices are more crucial than ever before.

Chapter 9. Non-Verbal Communication: A Silent Force in Group Dynamics

Non-verbal communication is often misunderstood, misinterpreted, or completely ignored, yet it is a powerful tool that, when harnessed effectively, can significantly enhance group dynamics.

9.1. Understanding Non-Verbal Communication

Our everyday interactions are filled with subtle non-verbal cues that often speak louder than words themselves. These non-verbal signals include facial expressions, body language, gestures, posture, eye contact, use of space, and even silence itself. They play a significant role in expressing emotions, attitudes, and information, often unintentionally, and can affect individual behavior and group dynamics.

Everyone uses non-verbal communication, but few truly understand its power. When paying attention to non-verbal signals, it's crucial to consider the cultural, social, and personal context in which they're expressed because their interpretations can differ widely across these variables.

9.2. The Role of Facial Expressions

Facial expressions are among the most powerful non-verbal cues. Consider the sheer depth of information that you can glean from someone's face: anxiety, happiness, disappointment, confusion, concentration, the list goes on. When harnessed correctly, understanding and interpreting these signals can significantly improve communication within a team.

For instance, as a team leader, noticing a look of confusion on a member's face during a strategy session may prompt you to ask if they understand or need further clarification. Such attentiveness to non-verbal cues not only fosters effective communication but encourages a culture of attentiveness and empathy, creating a more inclusive and supportive working environment.

9.3. Decoding Body Language

Body language includes posture, hand gestures, and overall body orientation. Gestures often complement verbal communication and can range from illustrative (like moving your hands to describe something) to symbolic (like a thumbs up for approval). Posture can express attentiveness, readiness, boredom, or openness, while the direction one faces can show interest or disinterest.

Reading body language accurately can significantly aid in understanding and interpreting team members' thoughts and feelings. For example, crossed arms may indicate defensiveness or discomfort, while leaning in generally shows interest.

9.4. Importance of Eye Contact

Eye contact is a significant channel of non-verbal communication. It can convey interest, attentiveness, respect, and even dominance, primarily depending on the duration and intensity. In a team setting, maintaining good eye contact when someone is speaking can indicate interest and respect for their thoughts and ideas while bolstering a sense of team unity and mutual respect.

9.5. Exploring the Use of Space

The concept of personal space or proxemics is another critical non-verbal communication aspect. Every individual has a different comfort level when it comes to their personal space. Encroaching on this space may make someone uncomfortable and defensive, while too much distance could be perceived as cold, aloof, or uninterested.

In a team context, finding a happy medium where everyone feels comfortable can encourage more open and effective communication. It includes not just personal spaces during conversations but also the layout and arrangement of team working spaces.

9.6. Leveraging Silence

Silence, an often-overlooked aspect of non-verbal communication, can be powerful. Pausing before responding can indicate respect for the speaker's thoughts. Using silence strategically can create emphasis, signaling the importance of the upcoming message.

In team communication, encouraging thoughtful silences instead of hasty responses can improve the quality of communication and decision-making.

9.7. Navigating Non-Verbal Communication in Virtual Teams

In an increasingly digital era, remote teams face the challenge of effectively interpreting non-verbal cues. Despite these limitations, non-verbal communication remains essential in virtual environments. Simple measures like using video conferencing for meetings and signals like thumbs up emojis or 'raise hand' features can partially compensate for the lack of in-person cues.

Mastering non-verbal communication is key to improving team communication. Remember, it's not about catching every non-verbal cue but about becoming more attuned to them to understand, interpret, and respond more effectively to your team.

Chapter 10. Cultivating Emotional Intelligence in Collaboration

Emotional intelligence is a critical aspect of effective communication and collaboration. It enables you to respond appropriately to others' emotions and to influence their responses. It involves four core skills: self-awareness, self-management, social awareness, and relationship management.

10.1. Knowing Yourself

To foster emotional intelligence in group collaboration, it's necessary first to understand oneself. Self-awareness involves understanding your own emotions and their impact on your actions and decision-making. Do you respond to stress by shutting down or lashing out? Which common workplace triggers provoke a strong emotional response? By recognizing these patterns, you can work towards controlling these behaviors that may impede group collaboration.

It's also important to assess personal strengths and weaknesses accurately. A poor self-perception results in either underestimating or overestimating abilities, affecting how you function within a group. On a regular basis, take some time to reflect on your emotions, behaviors, and their consequences.

10.2. Developing Self-Management

After developing self-awareness, the next step is self-management. This skill is about regulating your emotions to keep disruptive impulses in check and maintain productivity, even in tough circumstances. In the context of collaboration, self-management means handling internal conflicts and emotional reactions that could potentially harm group dynamics. Practice employing patience, adaptability, and integrity. Habits such as deep breathing, taking regular breaks, and positive affirmations can also support in managing emotional reactions.

10.3. Understanding Others

Good group collaboration invariably involves understanding others. Social awareness, another component of emotional intelligence, is all about empathy. To be empathetic, you need to develop a genuine understanding and appreciation of another person's emotions and perspective. This involves active listening, asking thoughtful questions, and validating others' feelings and ideas.

In an atmosphere of empathy, individuals feel heard, understood, and valued - a vital condition for effective collaboration. Frequently practice active listening in conversations by giving responses that indicate your understanding and avoiding interrupting while others are speaking.

10.4. Fostering Relationship Management

Relationship management is the ability to develop and maintain good relationships, communicate clearly, inspire and influence others, handle conflicts, and collaborate effectively. It is the end product of self-awareness, self-management, and social awareness. In the context of collaboration, it's about making every member feel part of the team and valued for their contributions.

You can build this skill through behaviors such as providing support to team members, competently handling and managing conflicts, and acknowledging others' input in group tasks. Maintaining open communication is critical, as it paves the path to trust and mutual respect.

10.5. Improving Emotional Intelligence

Emotional intelligence is not a fixed trait; you can develop and improve it over time. A few methods to cultivathe emotional intelligence include seeking feedback, practicing self-reflection, learning stress management techniques, and improving communication skills. Role-playing exercises, for instance, could be useful in practicing and improving emotional intelligence skills.

10.6. The Role of Emotional Intelligence in Collaboration

Emotional intelligence plays a significant role in collaboration. A team with high emotional intelligence can handle stress better, solve problems more efficiently, communicate effectively, and resolve conflicts without alienating team members. Such teams also exhibit empathy, appreciate diversity, and create a supportive, energizing work environment that enhances productivity.

In summary, cultivating emotional intelligence in collaboration is about developing the ability to manage your emotions and relationships effectively. It involves understanding oneself, managing your emotional reactions, appreciating others' perspectives, and fostering good relationships. Developing emotional intelligence is an ongoing process - an investment that promises significant rewards in terms of increased productivity and overall team satisfaction. Therefore, it's not just a worthy goal, but a critical component of excellent group collaboration.

Chapter 11. The Future of Group Communication: Trends to Watch

Understanding the future of group communication requires a keen awareness of emerging technologies, evolving social trends, and the increasing globalization of work teams. The future holds promising advancements that are likely to reshape the essence of team collaboration and redefine how we perceive group communication.

11.1. The Impact of Artificial Intelligence

The influence of Artificial Intelligence (AI) on group communication cannot be overstated. AI is poised to introduce automation in communication processes, thereby expediting information flow and reducing room for errors. NLP (Natural Language Processing) capabilities can enhance understanding among team members, dismantling language barriers and contributing to a more inclusive and diverse work environment.

Another game-changing AI innovation is the potential use of sentiment analysis tools. These tools can analyze a team's communication patterns to interpret the emotional climate of the group, allowing managers to intervene before conflicts escalate.

Furthermore, virtual assistants, powered by AI, can streamline scheduling, reminding, and even brainstorming sessions. Thus, we can expect an invigorated team environment with increased efficiency and reduced communication breakdowns.

11.2. Remote Work and Virtual Teams

With the proliferation of remote work, virtual teams are becoming the norm rather than the exception. Inclusive digital platforms that can accommodate teams spread across different time zones and cultural boundaries are apt to be essential group communication tools. These platforms must offer robust video conferencing facilities, real-time collaborative capabilities, and a seamless user experience to support the diverse requirements of a global team.

Moreover, considerations about connectivity, cybersecurity, and privacy are expected to drive improvements in virtual team communication tools. We may also witness a rise in the use of Virtual Reality (VR) and Augmented Reality (AR) to simulate in-person meetings, facilitating more realistic and immersive collaborative experiences.

11.3. Communication Training and Emotional Intelligence

The future of group communication is also likely to witness a surge in the importance of communication training and Emotional Intelligence (EI). As technologies evolve, teams must keep pace by learning new tools and unlearning obsolete habits. Regular training programs focusing on effective use of communication technology, managing virtual team dynamics, and enhancing interpersonal communication skills may become industry standards.

Developing EI within teams can promote empathy, foster mutual respect, and cultivate a more mindful communication environment. Teams with high EI are found to have less conflict, exhibit more positive group dynamics, and better problem-solving capabilities.

11.4. Transparency and Open Communication

As organizations continue to grapple with the fast-paced business environment, transparency is crucial to build trust amongst team members. A culture of open communication, where opinions are valued, mistakes are seen as learning opportunities, and decisions are made collectively is a trend we expect to solidify in the future. In such an environment, communication channels are likely to democratize further, flattening hierarchical communication lines.

11.5. The Rise of Asynchronous Communication

While real-time collaboration will always have its place, a trend towards asynchronous communication is emerging. This trend, influenced by the growing remote work culture, allows flexibility by accommodating diverse time zones and individual work rhythms. Correspondence tools allowing for delay feedback or responses encourage a thoughtful reflection over immediate reactions. This could lead to more meaningful contributions and a happier, more productive workforce.

In summary, the future of group communication beckons with promising opportunities. As teams evolve beyond traditional constraints and explore the vast potential of new technologies, they open avenues to unprecedented collaboration and creativity. With continuous learning and adaptability, teams can navigate these dynamic shifts, paving the way for a future where group communication becomes more efficient, inclusive, and impactful.

www.ingramcontent.com/pod-product-compliance
Lightning Source LLC
Chambersburg PA
CBHW071014260726
48661CB00007B/2960